The Ladies'
C H A M P

HOW TO DEFEAT THE ALLURE OF STRUGGLE LOVE

Carla Necole

ISBN: 978-0-578-29344-8

Acknowledgements

I want to thank YOU for purchasing this book.

And all the women who live unrepentant…you
showed me how to do it.

CONTENTS

Chapter One

THE DUST CHRONICLES

When you level up your self-esteem, realize your worth and stop being a male's emotional punching bag, you will be called a man hater, a feminist, a modern woman, or a misandrist.

I say if the stiletto fits, then wear it with pride. Preferably with a blade in the heel because these sickos will hurt you for not giving them your number.

Women have been groomed since we were little girls to be nice, stay pure, speak softly, to be a male's peace and to SUBMIT…all to get picked.

I am so glad that women are waking up and saying fuck that and fuck them.

Have you ever stopped to think why submission is being pushed so hard on us? Because it's NOT natural! It's not natural for a person to WANT TO BE oppressed.

When a male explains what submissive means, all I hear him saying is be non-challenging, overly tolerable and accepting of toxic behavior without complaint.

They also want you to cook, clean, sex, work, and shut up. See, I never could keep my mouth closed.

Even when I didn't know my worth, stayed in toxic relationships too long, and was afraid to ask the hard questions…I could never NOT curse your ass out.

This goes back to being feisty, yet still being in a fucked up situationship.

DO NOT ADVISE.

While he's demanding all these things, he's slinging community dick, has double-digit children by double-digit women, can't provide his part of the 50/50 finances that he demands, and doesn't help with the kids or around the house.

Then there's the other side of the coin…the male who has an education and makes six-figures. Yet still does all of the above, except he can pay his half. He also knows that his accomplishments are seen as rare, so he maintains a roster of women that he has no intention of committing to.

Like I said in chapter one…they are all swamp

things.

Both types, and any in between, use manipulation tactics to break a woman down versus pursuing the legions of women who believe their bullshit.

There are so many women who will bend into human pretzels to prove that she is that virtuous woman who deserves to get picked. She goes through great strains to remain docile and submissive despite never getting picked.

Or to only be picked by a male who uses her as a placeholder while he pursues the women he swears he can't stand.

If it's one thing males don't know…it's what they want.

Not only don't I care, but I also don't give a fuck. You shouldn't either. A woman should only be doing what makes her happy and what's true to her.

And that might not even include males.

I've been called a male hater who doesn't respect them. And all this is true to a certain extent.

I know mathematically that 100% of males aren't abusive, intolerable, non-likeable control freaks. But as a collective most of them are.

In my advocacy work with Human Trafficking

and Black Femicide, I know that caping for males is not in my best interests.

I pride myself on not being male-identified, and if a misogynistic thought surfaces (because the patriarchy has ruled since forever), I challenge and change that shit.

For me, this means not policing women's bodies, not holding women to male-identified views, not purity shaming women and not body shaming women…to name a few.

You'll never hear me say "a piece of a man is better than no man."

I don't let the asinine opinions of males sway me in any shape, form, or fashion. I laugh at these fools because their manipulation and gaslighting does NOT work over here.

I mean, consider the source, and how the "source" is the problem.

These views are from males who hate women, especially if we are intelligent and not easily persuaded.

These views are from males who hate women, especially if we are too independent to let them "lead" us straight to ruin.

These views are from males who hate women.

If he says that women talk too much, he means that women who TALK BACK to him are out of order. Because if you have your own opinion or stand up for yourself, you are a "bitch" to a controlling man.

This type of man thinks you are disrespecting him by not shutting up. He thinks that you are not worthy of talking back to him because you have a vagina. The penis-privileged think that having a penis makes them superior to women.

If he says you are too hard on males, he wants you to feel sorry for him for being weak-willed or mediocre. He's a self-proclaimed victim of life and a casualty of circumstance.

His life sucks because of the series of bad decisions he's made and continues to make. Yet, he wants you to overlook his irresponsibility, laziness, abusive characteristics, and selfishness.

At the end of the day, nothing is his fault, BUT you're still supposed to be grateful that he's there to give you trauma dick.

In other words, you are supposed to overlook his excuses and behavior, while maintaining his level of comfort, which he has done nothing to earn.

In all seriousness, he has no power over his life and should be left with his draws.

I had an ex once tell me that "you didn't even stick around to figure out what was wrong with me."

Listen, I'm not your mama, your minister, nor your magistrate. Go tell it on the mountain because you CANNOT tell it to me. Once my eyes were opened to the damage that the patriarchy has done to women, I vowed to never feel sorry for another penis person.

After all, they have created a society where women are treated as beneath them.

I once had an ex call me "pro-woman" in a condescending and dismissive way because every time he said something about women that I didn't like, I challenged him.

To him, me being confident, strong, and proud was overbearing. But nothing is said when men beat their chests, grab their balls and shout how superior they are ALL THE TIME.

Besides, if nobody else is pro-woman, a woman should be, right? Why wouldn't I be pro-myself? The biggest accomplishment of the patriarchy was to convince women not to stand up for our own best interests.

I am forever grateful that women can make their own money now. That we can get an education, buy our own homes, and vote for laws that benefit and protect us. If not for this, we'd be like our foremothers whose only escape was for their husbands to go off to war and die.

Some males believe that a woman's main goal

is to have her "one of him." He cannot fathom that a woman doesn't want his violent and abusive ass. He cannot comprehend when a woman is not interested in a one-sided relationship.

We've all heard about a male's ego and how he needs to feel superior. Well, we need to feel good about ourselves too. Therefore, do not downplay your accomplishments or your intelligence to make a male feel "bigger." Let him get a penis pump for that.

I once had an ex tell me that I always had to be the smartest person in the room. What he meant was "when you speak on a subject that I know nothing about, you must be trying to make me feel small."

Listen, it is not my fault that reading is not a priority for you.

Next up is "you think you're better than me." He hopes that saying this will prompt you to work harder to stroke his ego. This is him trying to keep you in your place by putting you on the defense.

If the way you carry yourself is a threat to his insecure ass, then so be it.

As a matter of fact, prove to him that you are better by not giving him another second of your time. Gracefully bow out and let him play mind games with his mama.

And then there's "no other man will ever love you like I do." While using my analytical mind, I determined that this is a good thing. When his "love" comes with lots of lying and cheating, who would want to be "loved" like that again.

I recently saw a story where a serial baby-maker gave his teenage daughter a "purity" ring.

So, it's okay for you to create broken homes all over your greater tri-state area, but you want to shame your daughter into 'saving herself.'

The gag is if women stay pure how will his kind continue to create kids to abandon? Hypocrisy is indeed the foundation of the dust chronicles.

They use different tactics to keep you in the relationship pits. They want you to think that you can't do better, so that you will stick with males on the sub-zero level.

I saw yet another post where this guy said how he wanted to date an exotic black woman (who isn't African American) who speaks more than one language and has zero kids.

His own qualifications were African American, uneducated (witnessed by his sub-par language and grammar skills) and multiple kids by multiple women. I kid you not (pun intended). He was obviously hypocritical

AND delusional.

What beautiful, educated, and well-cultured woman of any ethnicity would be checking for him? Stop letting these males who have nothing to offer besides defunct sperm play in your face.

Here's a list of other males to never speak to nor procreate with:

Males who think that what a woman wears or does for a living deserves to be raped. I can wear a mini skirt and be a sex worker. That does not entitle you to my body. If he thinks like this, he's a rapist.

Some folks with vaginas believe this too, so keep yourself, your sisters, your daughters, and your nieces away from them as well.

Hoteps who are "fake woke," overbearing, homophobes who spew uneducated respectability politics that are very harmful to women. A hotep can ho-step his ass away from me. Go pursue the women who side with you and leave the rest of us in dustless peace.

Males who are overly concerned about the last time you had sex are predatory and rapey. If a man asks you this, the next thing he should hear is the dial tone, and possibly police sirens. Block him from every avenue of communication known to humankind. I'd even consider getting him added to the sex offender registry.

I recently saw on social media where a guy called a woman childish because she said she doesn't have sex on the first date. This coming from a demographic who are easier to bag than groceries. On the one hand, they want to gaslight you into purity. While on the other hand, they want to be the one to defile you. This had date rape written all over it.

A male always talking about his penile appendage makes me want to vomit. Who wants to hear you lie about the orgasms you didn't cause? Like bring something to the table other than your genitalia, sir. As a matter of fact, you ruined it, I'd rather talk to (and have sex with) a gray rock. And yes, you're giving me rape vibes.

I maintain that being married or having a man should not be a woman's priority. Historically, they have objectified, disregarded, and abused women to maintain their power and privilege.

I do, however, understand the desire for companionship and partnership. I know that although you don't need a male, you might want one.

You will never see me teaching ladies how to find or keep a male. You will always see me teaching women how to love themselves, validate themselves and get their own money.

You will see me teaching what red flags to look out for and how self-preservation should be your top priority.

Beware of the dust chronicles.

Thoughts...

_____

_____

_____

_____

_____

_____

_____

_____

_____

_____

_____

_____

_____

_____

_____

_____

_____

_____

_____

_____

_____

_____

_____

_____

PARABLE OF A BAD FIXER-UPPER

One day as I was pumping gas, a homeless guy walked up on me and asked for some change. I only had $0.37 (you read that right thirty-seven cents) in my cup holder and he proudly held out his hand. And that's not even the worst part of this story.

This is…

AFTER he took one quarter, one dime and two pennies he had the unmitigated gall to ask for my phone number. Before I was just disgusted, but now I was offended.

This, ladies, was when I realized that AUDACITY IS HOMELESS.

I've heard grandiose tales of women taking

males off the streets, cleaning them up and the male becomes a preacher.

I can see homelessness being a prerequisite for ministry, so the career choice kind of makes sense.

However, I would NEVER rescue a homeless male OR marry a preacher. Both sound miserable to me.

But some folks would call this "relationship goals" or "true love" or a "success story." I call it the desperation of a woman who has drunk the "it's better to have a piece of a man than no man" Kool-Aid.

Women are often shamed into giving unworthy males ridiculous chances, with the hope of her gamble paying off. But just like the lottery, you're not going to hit 99.9% of the time.

Taking in a homeless person is akin to taking in a rabid coyote, because you thought it was just an ugly puppy. It's not an ugly puppy, it's a predator and somebody (most likely you) will get bitten.

I know these were extreme examples, but the point I'm trying to make is to stop dating a male's potential.

I'm about 100% sure that MOST women have dated a male based solely on his "potential progression percentage" or "PPP" if you will.

That's my cute way of saying that MOST women have dated a male who had absolutely no proof of life progression.

The most common cause of this is "fairy-tale thinking" and 30-minute sitcoms.

You commit yourself to an IDEA of what you THINK he can become versus what is staring you in the face with feral eyes. And you hope he is as ambitious about your future together as you are.

Whether he sold you a dream, or you paid for it with credit, you are banking your future on his potential ability to become a worthy partner.

Potential does not equal to a possible relationship, and many a woman has worn her patience, time, and money thin by not knowing the difference.

If a man is of the age to be established, then he should be so. His growth and evolution should have happened long before you two crossed paths.

Once a woman is of a certain age, it is foolish to still be "dating his potential."

Aren't your nerves bad enough with all the grown woman shit you're doing?

Let me say right here and right now that I KNOW that not all women aspire to be somebody's wife or partner. Nor do I think "finding a man" should be a priority for any woman. It's NOT for me.

Many women, however, do want to be married, are actively dating, or are single and want to make better choices in the future. I respect a woman's desires. Period.

Therefore, regardless of where you are on the dating spectrum, I am vehemently against you dating someone's potential.

And as always, I speak from cold hard experience. Dating "potential" is dating an imaginary person who may or may not EVER show up in real life. Despite what a person has, or has accomplished, date them for who they are presently.

Or risk being greatly disappointed. Over and over again.

Building together means more than ONE person contributing to a common goal. If one person is established, and the other person only has potential, then who is really building?

Your load will not be lighter in any way by dating someone's potential.

The only thing that WILL be lighter is your bank account and your mental reserves because he won't be bringing anything to the table.

I'm not interested in pulling up anybody's bootstraps. I AM interested in pulling up my own big girl panties and fulfilling my own potential.

This is important because by taking charge of YOUR life, you will recognize which step of the process a male is in and be able to proceed accordingly.

A lot of times how you grew up is relevant to how you behave in relationships. In other words, the way you related to your mama or daddy…is the way you relate towards a romantic partner.

Your attachments to dead weight are even worse if you had a "flawed" parent that you tried to save or fix. As an adult, your "savior behavior" tricks you into being attracted to males who need you to be Captainess Save-a-hoe.

You're never going to save him because you can only save yourself. The psychology behind this is that while you're trying to "fix" him… you are hoping that you get fixed too.

After all, the greatest romantic fantasy is to heal together and conquer all odds, also known as, struggle love. Never get caught up in the "us against the world" struggle.

That void that you are trying to fill through your partner is often linked to your family's dysfunctional dynamics. Neither your parents, nor your partner, is your problem to fix.

So, you can let go of any obligation, guilt, or shame.

These three have no place in a healthy and loving relationship.

Let your desire to love yourself outweigh your desire to love someone else, and get the healing that you need.

I used to not understand when people said that our relationships were a reflection of us.

I would legit get mad because I knew that I wasn't the type of person who would purposely try to destroy anyone physically, mentally, or financially.

I also knew that I wasn't an exploitative person who used up people's energy or funds.

Therefore, I wasn't trying to hear all that "he's your mirror" psychobabble.

It took me years to figure out that in this sense, "reflection" meant trying to fill a void from childhood wounds. That's the ONLY correlation you should accept when looking inward for answers to your relationship patterns.

THAT MUTHAFUCKA IS NOT YOUR LITERAL MIRROR AND YOU NEVER DESERVED HIS ABUSE.

For example, you may feel the need to help someone undeserving because, despite all your flaws, someone loved you at your worst.

You may feel like it's your purpose to save someone because, despite all your childhood fears, no one came to save you.

You might even feel like you need to fix someone's problems because, when you were little, no one tried to soothe your pain.

You want to give him the love, attention, and safety that you deserved growing up but did not get.

In other words, you understand the hurt kid that is inside someone else. More accurately, you SEE the hurt kid in someone else.

And because you are empathetic to this pain you feel sorry for the male with a weak potential progression percentage (PPP).

Well, NOT ANYMORE! Never feel bad for the penis privileged. They have the upper hand in society JUST BECAUSE they have a dick.

If even they can't figure out how to save themselves, then you don't have a snowball's chance in hell.

Okay?

Choose a different ministry! The ministry of YOU.

You must be SAVAGE about your heart and your mind. You cannot continue to martyr yourself for a bad fixer upper.

You know what all martyrs have in common? They're dead!

Martyrdom in relationships is placing one's happiness above your own. It's taking the blame for someone else's misery. It's taking on all the financial responsibilities because he hasn't reached his potential yet. Martyrdom is selling yourself short.

Again…

All. Martyrs. Are. Dead.

His shit is not yours to flush.

The first step is becoming aware enough to know if a person is causing an unhealthy need in you. This may take therapy if you had a very traumatic childhood or a series of abusive relationships.

The second step is being strong enough to act accordingly, which usually means leaving his ass with his draws.

If you think your love can save him, ask yourself these questions:

How many times have you hoped this hope before? What metrics or proof are you basing this on? How did it work out in the end?

No matter how hard you love someone, they will NOT change until they are ready to do so. Consider how hard it is to change yourself and you will see that it's impossible to change someone else.

Likewise, you cannot love him into his potential. If you want to save yourself some heartache stop dating his potential and accept his reality instead.

Your little "spidey sense (intuition)" is tingling with doubt, and each day brings more anxiety, because deep down you know he's already reached his lukewarm potential.

When will we start putting some respect on our intuition? For intuition is the remedy for delusions.

It's telling you that you made a mistake dating a guy with potential (again). Everything he does (and doesn't do) starts grating on your nerves. You start mumbling and grumbling to your girls about his "lack of ambition." As it turns out, he's not complex, he's just shiftless.

And let me just drop this right here, right now. An active addict (of any kind) does not make for a potential partner. Unless you are a clinician, you cannot help. And if you are a clinician, don't use "dating" them as a synonym for helping them.

Unfortunately, we can also be bamboozled by a highly effective "potential perp." Also known as the high-value male.

He seems like the type who goes after what he wants with no regard for social acceptability.

But what is he really getting done?

All his "struggling to get free" talk is most likely smoke being blown up your arse in the name of civil liberties.

Sometimes "potential" just means "no talent." Just because he's self-deceived doesn't mean you have to be. Make choices based on what IS versus what is imagined.

For instance, if he's an artist, then where is the damn art?

Is he planning or just playing? A plan has actionable steps, measurable goals, and practical deadlines. If there's no plan, then tell him that playtime is over.

It's not about what he says because he will say ANYTHING to get what he wants. It must be about what he DOES. And there needs to be evidence of DOING. And signs of progression.

And let me tell you something else, waiting around for him to reach his potential is stifling your own. You're so busy sowing into his fallacies that you aren't living your best life.

What deposits have you sown into your own dreams lately? What actions have you taken to inflate your dollars? How are you currently "GOAL digging?" Who is supporting your efforts to bear fruit?

If you are dating "potential," then I bet your answers to those questions are quite disappointing to you.

It is draining to be in a relationship when you are channeling YOUR potential into saving someone else.

In your quest for world domination (or just a better life), it is important to partner with someone who is already established in their own right.

If you want to build a sustainable and supportive relationship (or legacy), it is important to partner with someone who is already FULFILLING potential.

Dating someone's potential USUALLY equates to dating someone with lots of ideas and lots of issues. But with the lack of a plan, focus or drive.

There may be some exceptions to the rule, but we don't care, because we're not willing to risk it, right?

Stop dating potential and date someone who is already winning with potential.

Because when you bend over backwards for a male, he will bend forward for you to kiss his ass.

Thoughts...

_____

_____

_____

_____

_____

_____

_____

_____

_____

_____

_____

_____

_____

_____

_____

_____

_____

_____

_____

_____

_____

_____

_____

Chapter Three

NOW, I AM SAYING HE'S A GOLD DIGGER

Although Kanye West didn't start this obsession with identifying gold diggers, he DID give losers the cojones to use it without just cause.

Gold digger is a misogynistic noun that men created so that women would not ask them for money, or for financial help.

You see, they decided at the annual "sucka summit" that they did not want to be held accountable for anything that cost, which is everything.

Okay, I made the summit up, but doesn't it seem like they get together to rehearse? They literally say the same shit verbatim.

Gold digging became a very popular way to shame women as males refused to step up financially.

The idea of gold digging is an ignorance doctrine perpetuated by "chump change males" so that you expect nothing from them.

When I say chump change, I mean no assets, no savings, no retirement plan, and no gold to dig for.

They accuse us of digging for gold that is invisible. It doesn't exist and it never did. They know there's no gold.

They are training you to not expect anything from them because they know they will never be able to provide it.

But instead of bettering themselves, they become wizards and try to make you believe in magic; like they had some money and then poof it was gone.

He NEVER had it!

It is also used by men who date out of their league physically, but have the funds to wine, dine and spoil.

However, when the woman is done with his ass, or starts dating someone she actually likes, deputy dumb starts screaming how "she's a gold digger!"

Listen, "a fair exchange ain't no robbery." You bought her time because you knew you had no business with her in the first place. Males think that they have a monopoly on having preferences.

They don't!

You have every reason to expect gifts, accept favor and STILL hold out for what you really want. They do it all the time.

I laugh in their faces when the rules of the patriarchy backfire on them. After all, they made the rules. They just never expected women to become empowered enough to use the rules to their advantage.

Now, here's what I found while searching the term "gold digger," on Google's first page:

1 the term "gold digger" is used to refer to a woman who associates herself with wealthy men purely for monetary benefits.

2 a woman who associates with or marries a man chiefly for material gain.

3 gold diggers can be defined as a woman whose main reason for hooking up is so that they can gain material benefits from the latest sponge they're dating.

4 a person who dates others purely to extract money from them, in particular, a woman who strives to marry a wealthy man.

There are many more definitions, and they all point a dirty-nailed, callused finger at women.

Oh, the ramifications here are clear!

A gold digger is a scheming and predatory woman, who breathes dollar signs like a dragon breathes fire. And takes males to the proverbial financial cleaners.

Sadly, this narrative has worked on many women because she doesn't want to be called a gold digger. They become so afraid to ask for help, or that a man at least holds his own, that it's a Shakespearean tragedy.

Yet, women continue to try to make males see them as "different" from the rest. This had got to stop.

Males, on the other hand, don't care what they are called as they use women up, eat up the kid's snacks, play video games all night, cheat all day while the woman is at work and contribute zero dollars and zero cents to the household.

They are capitalizing off women with no feelings of remorse.

They use the fact that you don't expect anything from them to their advantage. They get all kinds of perks from you: your time, your money, your sex. While contributing little to nothing in return.

Honestly, the women I grew up watching were the opposite of gold diggers. They held their families down, shouldered all the stress and made unreasonable sacrifices for the people they loved.

In fact, they were coal-diggers:

Coal diggers deliberately select partners whose attractiveness lies in the fact that they are a financial liability. More simply put, they chose males who didn't have the pot, the piss, or the window.

They chose bums.

I got coal digger from google too, and the first thing I noticed is that the definition specifies that a "man or woman" can be a coal digger.

But in the gold digger definitions they called out only women.

I find it ironic (sarcasm) that gold digger is a term primarily relegated to women.

However, when it comes to long-suffering with broke dusties, the men get to be victims as well.

I know many women who are homeowners, degree holders, have professional careers and are financially independent.

Sadly, a lot of these same women take on the additional responsibility of birthing an adult male specimen.

They get with males who dare to fix their mouths to call you a gold digger if you expect them to hold their own or make your life a little easier.

Now, how can you dig for gold in a barren ass cave? There's nothing to dig for.

One thing I know about a woman who takes care of her business is this:

You don't have time for frivolous excursions like digging for imaginary gold. As you are busy taking care of your home, yourself, your career, your family, and your kids.

The idea of you being a gold digger is another self-serving double standard to keep you giving more and expecting less.

It's NOT okay for him to move into your house, drive your car, eat your food, and bring all his kids. It IS okay for you to expect room and board, cost of living and daycare fees.

I constantly see women dating beneath them. It started with me seeing it in myself.

Yes, I'm telling the truth about the seeing and the doing. I think it's a problem that many women can relate to.

It's NOT normal for every male you date to have no permanent residence, have no reliable transportation, and have no place of employment.

It IS normal for you to say, "you're out of your league." If you're afraid to say it (because some of them will kill you for rejecting them) then at least keep it moving like a runaway train.

Comically, there are multiple articles to teach males how to spot a gold digger, and what to do if he does. I swear I'm not making this up.

So, I thought I'd even the playing field a little and help the ladies out.

1 The only time he has his "own place" is when he is living with a woman. Otherwise, he is living with his mom in the same room he grew up in. He doesn't have enough gold to pay rent.

2 Every time you're on your way to see him, he asks you to stop at the wing shack to get him the highest chicken-to-fry-combo. But when he comes to your house, he always has one meal, just enough for him. He didn't even tell you he was stopping to get something to eat. He doesn't have enough gold to pay for your food.

3 He is always spending the night at your house until you mention the bill that you just got out of the mailbox. Then he stays at his moms for a few nights until you "forget" you mentioned it. He doesn't have enough gold to contribute to a bill.

4 His first conversations with you are about his financial limitations "right now" and how women who don't understand a man's plight

31

are shallow and selfish. He doesn't have any gold.

5 He complains about high maintenance women and thinks it's stupid for women to waste their money on certain "luxuries" (like hair and shoes, but NEVER Jordans because he wants some a pair of those himself). He doesn't have enough gold to provide for your upkeep.

6 He thinks that since you earn more than him, his money should be the "fun" money, and not go toward bills. After all, you were paying them by yourself before he got there. He is correct so kick his ass to the curb and do good by yourself. Plot twist, he doesn't have enough money for fun either.

7 He asks for "healthy" loans to buy a car or to get his mama a Mother's Day gift. Somehow you never get paid back. He never mentions it again and counts on all that "forgetting" that you are doing. You also never see said car nor gift. He doesn't have enough gold to pay you back.

8 He brings you gifts "hot" off the streets that he bartered for in cigarettes. But expects you to purchase him the latest "brand new" game console with money you worked for. He doesn't have enough gold to buy you gifts.

9 He expects you to be grateful for any little effort that he half-assedly makes. For instance,

you complain because you shoveled snow out the driveway while he was snoring. He comes back with "Well, didn't I get up on Tuesday to warm up your car?" But it's Friday now and he only got up AFTER you cleared the snow. He has ALL the audacity.

10 He has a "baby I want this" list for every occasion: His birthday, Xmas, President's Day. But he's going to get you something too. Can you guess what it is? It's the same thing he always gets you, silly. You get "The D." He has ALL the free dick.

If I've said it once, I've said it a thousand times! There is nothing wrong with you wanting a partner who has as much as, OR MORE THAN you do.

Males who are on the same mental wavelength as you will get this. There is a difference between building together on a solid foundation and gold digging.

There is something wrong with letting dusty bums use you for your resources with no intention of lightening your load in any way.

Not only do these men deplete your resources, but they are energy vampires as well. He won't wash the car, gas it up or fix a damn thing on it.

He won't cut the grass, fix the toilet, or change a blown light bulb.

He won't cook a meal, take you out or even pick up fast food.

Listen, if you feel uncomfortable leveling up, then at least stick with someone on your same level. But never ever settle for less again.

Stop caring so much about what a male thinks about you, especially when it's to the detriment of your own preservation.

It is not your fault that he is a career criminal and can't get a good job. He shouldn't have broken the law.

It is not your fault that he has eleven kids and is dodging child support. He should have been more responsible with his penile appendage.

It is not your fault that he is broke. See numbers one and two.

It is not your responsibility to carry his load or to feel sorry for him.

When you are down and depressed, he thinks "she will figure it out…she always does."

Give him that same benefit of the doubt. You need to stop feeling guilty for how far behind he is in life.

No one taught me how to go to college, budget my money or buy a house in my 20's. No one makes me take care of my son or pay my bills.

Yes, I learned a lot of lessons through trial and error. Yes, I learned about relationships the hard way. Yes, I've made a lot of mistakes along the way.

But I learned. You learned too. Now it's his turn. He is not entitled to what you have worked hard for.

Males have gender privilege, so it's their fault when they fumble the bag. They've always had better opportunities and got to do everything first (go to college, get a mortgage, WORK, vote).

Never let chump change call you a gold digger!

Like most current patriarchal and sexist terms, "gold digger" is a made-up word used to keep women "in their place" and not expecting much.

"In our place" to them means being sexually repressed, stupidly submissive and settling for any man for the sake of having one.

As more women start to realize the societal games that the patriarchy plays, you'll feel less embarrassed and more pissed off.

YOU have to look out for YOU because in our society you're damned if you do and damned if you don't.

Start seeking your own level...like water does.

I would be remiss if I didn't leave you with some of my petty (at least it's true).

35

Males are the original gold diggers. Traditionally, it was males who sought plentiful dowries (money) when looking for a wife.

They sought out girls and women who had wealthy families to fatten their pockets and increase their standing in society.

It only became a BAD thing once women started seeking financial security through wealthier husbands.

They cannot stand when we wise up. They need us to stay beneath them so that they can feel superior.

When they try to put you in your place, remind them that your place is AT THE TOP!

Thoughts...

_____
_____
_____
_____
_____
_____
_____
_____
_____
_____
_____
_____
_____
_____
_____
_____
_____
_____
_____
_____
_____
_____

QUIZ: THE DOLLAR DUCHESS

Where do you stand with your money?

Quiz directions:

* Answer "yes" or "no" to the following 20 questions (takes less than 3 minutes)

* Add up the number of times you said "yes"

* Read your results

Do you often wonder why 'bad' or 'evil' people seem to prosper the most?

Does it seem to you that selfish people are the ones who consistently get ahead in life?

Do you feel like you could never be wealthy no matter what you do?

Do you ask yourself, "If there is enough for everyone, why is there poverty, homelessness and starvation?"

Do you wonder "If it's so easy to make money, why are so few people wealthy?"

Do you believe that more poor people will make it to heaven than rich people?

Do you think to yourself "I think about money all the time, so why don't I attract more of it?"

Do you feel like you deserve to earn more than you earn right now?

Does having a steady paycheck feel like financial security (because at least money is coming in)?

Do you feel like most wealthy people have luck on their side?

Do you believe that hard work and sacrifice is the key to riches?

Do you feel like money comes to you easily?

Do you think that money changes people for the worse?

Do you feel that a characteristic flaw (i.e. laziness) hinders your success?

Do you feel like you never win anything?

Do you believe that a lack of knowledge is holding you back from success?

Do you feel like there is that one person or opportunity that would open the floodgates of prosperity for you?

Would you rather live comfortably rather than be rich?

Should you be financially rewarded for helping others?

Should you be grateful with what you have, and not expect more?

If you answered "yes" to 1-3 questions...

You are ambitious, highly successful in your own right, and you have experienced above-average potential, but you are dissatisfied.

You may be an inconsistent earner.

You make a decent income but you want more, and know deep-down that you are not paid your worth.

You may even be working a job that you want to move away from.

If you answered "yes" to 4-6 questions…

You likely have some outdated beliefs regarding money, your access to it and your ability to earn more of it.

You feel like a mediocre earner, you watch your peers up-level, and wonder why your life is still the same.

You may sometimes make small financial advances, only to have a setback, so that you never really break through to the success you want and deserve.

If you answered "yes" to 7-10 questions…

You most likely have an unhealthy desperation with money that makes it feel out of reach to you.

You may live check-to- check and earn just enough to get by. You feel guilty if you even get up the nerve to splurge on yourself.

You're scared to step out of your comfort zone and take a risk because you're afraid that you will end up worse off than when you started.

If you answered "yes" to 11-20 questions...

You may be headed to, or already experiencing, severe financial challenges.

No amount of financial advice or budgeting plan seems to work for you.

You are in a 'cycle of victimization' where you feel like life works against you.

You have judgments about money and people with a lot of money. These judgments may be so deep that you don't realize them, but the proof is in your bank account.

Chapter Four

"JUST SAY NO!" TO NICE

If there's one muthafucka you need to be leery of, it's "Mr. Nice Guy (MNG)."

Of course, there are others you should avoid like a plague of locusts, like "only a face his mother could love," "can I get a hug," and "what do you bring to the table."

But we'll start with "MNG" because he is usually the one who's been waiting in the shadows for your lopsided and toxic ass relationship to crash and burn.

He'll gaslight you by saying you keep overlooking the nice guys (he's talking about himself) and therefore you deserve dusty male behavior.

The thing I hate most about "MNG" is that he plays the long game. For years, he has covertly manipulated experiences with you that should happen organically if there is real chemistry.

You may have discussed boundaries, but MNG ignores them because it's not what he wants to hear. Therefore, he tries to sneakily find a way around them.

For example, you make it clear that you never plan on having sex with him. However, he waits until you're vulnerable to try and have sex with you anyway. He's abusive and predatory. No gray area.

He wants you to ignore the fact that you feel no attraction to him because he thinks that being nice should be the remedy for lack of attraction.

The penis people don't settle on their attraction preferences, and neither should we. His preferences are why he's in your face right now knowing good and well that he's out of his league.

He's trying to covertly convince your fine ass to make a decision that feels ugly to you.

He'll temporarily put your wants and needs before his own because he thinks his sacrifices will put you in a position where you cannot refuse his advances.

To me this shows that MNG has no qualms about forcing his will on you. He doesn't care about manipulating your body or matters of the heart. He is truly a predator.

He's hiding who he really is. He thinks that

hiding his mistakes, and other things you may dislike, will leave you nothing to criticize. He wants you to think that he'd be perfect if only he wasn't so unattractive.

These males know that we are taught to overlook how they look, how they provide and how promiscuous they are. While we are taught to always look good, stay in shape, and keep our body count low.

They use this sexist doctrine to their advantage, which is why they have the audacity to try dating out of their league in the first place.

He knows that he's not your first, second or third choice. But he's going to play nice until he sees his opportunity to strike like the serpent that he is.

How does he know he'll have an opportunity to strike? Because he also knows that collectively, males are the problem.

He knows that there's a good chance that the guy you are currently dating is going to mess it up.

The dating pool is ACTUALLY a swamp. So even if you DO get away from the alligator, the other creatures are dangerous as well. Because they are all still swamp things.

Males know this, even if they try to make you think it's your fault that your dating history has been trash. He thinks victim-blaming will make you doubt yourself enough to give his trash ass a try.

Which brings me to my next point…

NEVER GIVE THEM PITY PUSSY. If he's not attractive enough to get the woman he wants the old-fashioned way, then he can get her the OLD-old-fashioned way. He can pay for it.

Although paying a sex worker would save him a lot of time and rejection, he'd rather play mind games and wait you out like 'cat and mouse.'

Why? Because he gets a kick out of wearing you down or witnessing you do something you said you'd never do (him). And most males think they are entitled to have the body of any woman they lust after.

It's sick, but true.

Although he comes off as nice, he's really an angry little troll (ALT), and he's irritated because he's been restricting his disgusting behaviors and you haven't rewarded him yet.

He wants to be rewarded with sex if you haven't figured that out already.

Remember, the only reason he's hiding his true self is because he thinks being MNG will trick you into lowering your standards and desiring him.

What does the term "nice" even mean? After

all, it's a subjective personality trait and it's not even measurable. You can turn on being nice at any time. Most of us do this effortlessly throughout our day.

Yes, it's important to pay attention to how people treat others on the regular, but a person's character tells the true tale.

I grew up around toxic and aggressive men who were the ultimate abusers of women. But you could bet your next paycheck that they could be nice. They could even be downright charming.

This duality of nasty and nice is what keeps women hooked in these abusive relationships in the first place. So, of course, a master manipulator has perfected his strategy through repetition and effort.

MNG is also a master manipulator who tries to be whoever you want him to be. This facade may weaken your defenses and cause you to ignore the fact that you don't want him.

He may present himself as non-sexual, or as having great self-control, because he wants you to think that he doesn't objectify you like other guys do.

This is reverse psychology at its most 'pitiful-ness.' He's thinking, "if she thinks I don't want sex from her, I have more of a chance of having sex with her."

When you've stuck to your guns long enough and he still hasn't persuaded you in his favor, his dusty essence will emerge.

He'll say you must like jerks or bad boys because you don't like him. This is misogynistic behavior, because it stems from the stereotype that women want to be dominated and controlled.

Although he's throwing shit and hoping it sticks, he's not willing to examine himself. He refuses to entertain the notion that there are other reasons you have passed him up.

He uses his "MNG" status as leverage to get what he wants, or as evidence that he deserves what he wants.

We are taught as girls not to hurt boy's feelings so that we can be chosen. This is sometimes taught with intention, and sometimes we learn it through our environment.

We've seen our granny, mothers, and aunts bite their tongues or play dumb to make a male feel superior or in control.

It's time for women to stop people-pleasing, stop the male worship and to get off the struggle love bus for good! A penis does not make one superior.

Don't care about his feelings if he is pressuring you into a situation you don't want to be in. Stick to your guns and watch how MNG switches up on you. I've seen it. I've heard it.

He'll use any pain point you shared with him against you. Because he feels rejected, he will now try to tear you down. He's gone from begging you for a chance, to reminding you of your insecurities.

He's angry because he suffers from serial rejection, and a perpetual inability to attract the women he sexually covets.

IF you give this type a chance, he WILL start playing "the dating games." These are like the hunger games, but not as clever or sensational.

It will become his mission to make you want him so that he can turn the tables and reject you back.

And this is why you can't even stick him in the friend zone. Just send him to the abyss of no more.

Let's just do away with the friend zone altogether, shall we?

If he's friend-zoned too long, pursuing you becomes all about revenge. You'll see signs of aggression, agitation, and hostility. He never wanted to be friends anyway. He ALWAYS wanted to have sex with you.

Your yoni is not a consolation prize, nor is it a bargaining chip. Trust me, you don't need him riding in to rescue your vagina. Ye shall be disappointed.

MNG thinks that he is rare. Maybe he means like a carcass. Which kind of makes sense if you think about it; raw, undone, cold.

I digress…

This fool is trying to use the 'fear of scarcity' tactic on you to make you think you are missing out on something good. You know the same tricks business marketers use to get you to BUY NOW!

They'll usually tell you that you'll die alone and barren with a multitude of cats.

Do not fall for this. Your biological clock will tick longer than his dick will dick. While we are in our prime years, males are on the decline. They are needing penile enhancements in their 20's and 30's and they die alone more than we do.

Plus, this "you're going to die an old cat lady" narrative is so tired that I took a nap while writing it. Every seasoned woman that I know whose husband died (even if it was 40 years ago) did not get remarried. Women have wizened up and know that males are a liability to us more so than assets.

Those old-fashioned values that they "remind" us that our grandmothers had, weren't values at all. They were survival skills. Our foremothers HAD to rely on males for survival because they couldn't work, have a bank account or mortgage, get an education, and couldn't vote at one point.

And the males back then weren't nice either. They raped their wives, beat them into submission and had multiple families across town or across the street.

Males were able to do everything first, and still managed to fumble the bag. This is the real reason they are scrambling to brainwash us into "needing" them again.

They know that financial independence affords us a level of freedom from their dust chronicles.

You have more options. And we are quicker to leave him with his drawers.

You deserve love without suffering for it first.

Thoughts...

Chapter Five

MIND YOUR GENITALS, DON'T LET'EM MIND YOU

I don't know about you, but I was once the "good" girl who was attracted to "bad" boys.

By good I mean I did what was expected of me.

Despite growing up in a violent neighborhood and home, I breezed through elementary, middle, and ended high school with a bang as Valedictorian.

I was the first in my immediate family to go to college, then I went on to get a graduate degree. Yep, I got degreed up because I was taught that THAT would be the way out of poverty.

Although I grew up in the projects, I'd like to think that I skipped cutely down the proverbial yellow-brick-road and right into urban suburbia.

But my journey wasn't linear, nor did my story unfold like I was told it would. That story was to go to college, get a good job, have 2.5 kids, and live the good ole American dream.

I was willing to do all of that too, except for the 2.5 kids. But what had happened was student loans, low-paying jobs, and a recession.

Despite having an MBA, I worked for peanuts for many years. I was even laid off twice in a five-year span. I did have a son (1.5 kids short) when I was in my early 30's, but not by any knight in any shining armor.

I was more like a cockroach in rusted tinfoil.

And don't even get me started on the grad-school-debt versus cost-of-living ratio, also known as debt, that you can't see your way out of.

Instead of saving me from poverty, grad school put me further down the economic ladder.

Nevertheless, I was intelligent, independent, and resourceful.

But when it came to dating, I was imbecilic, irresponsible, and just really really bad at it.

One day my sister said, "good girls always like bad boys," referring to me as the good girl. Of course, I'd heard the expression before, but never in reference to me.

I believe this is called being in denial.

In hindsight, I should have reflected on what she'd said more, but I saw it as dating something I was familiar with, which at that time was the bottom of the barrel.

I was still in the idealistic "give folks a chance" stage. The "you're no better than anyone else" stage. Basically the "settling stage."

No matter the stage, the "good girl, bad boy" fiasco still happens to this day. And I'm going to tell you why.

Bad boys have the so-called swag for days, which means they are mysterious, dark, and dangerous. Or they are the vintage bad boy who lives fast and free.

Ladies, this bad boy persona is another skewed view that we learned from TV, and possibly hip-hop music.

Bad boys are never a good idea.

Yes, he's broody and dangerous. Not because he's a deep thinker, but because he's constantly keeping you guessing about your place in his life.

Or lack thereof because days, weeks and months may go by before you hear from him again.

A bad boy is a renegade who believes that

rules are made to be broken.

And he's broken a few laws too. But his recklessness is attractive to a woman who (a) grew up with nothing but these types of men around her or (b) has never met a man like this and the newness is intoxicating.

Every male I'd grown up around was a bad boy.

At first, I wasn't so hung up on the "why" of why I was attracted to bad boys. I didn't even know it was a negative pattern for me at the time. I just thought "I like what I like," and "you can't help who you fall in love with."

Well, you do like what you like, but it's important to like what's healthy for you. I mean, I love Coca-Cola and have a love/hate relationship with water. I'm not ready to admit which is better for me yet.

Okay, it's water!

And "you can't help who you fall in love with" is a lie and a myth. It's straight bullshit with no chaser. If you never open yourself up to a certain type, then you won't run the risk of falling for them.

Because you CAN love someone for all the wrong reasons. Reasons that are detrimental to you.

Even though I wasn't fully aware of the "why," as one relationship crashed after another, I had to start paying attention to my patterns and behaviors.

I realized that I felt comfy with the bad boy type as this type of man was all I'd seen or experienced.

My dating habits were in fact a byproduct of my environment. This realization was painful to me at first, because I thought I was too smart to be so stupid.

I mean, I'd gotten out of the projects, gone to college, and broken the poverty cycle in my family. I was a homeowner at 26 years as a single woman and constantly bettering myself.

Yet, I was still dating males who were beneath me in important areas of life.

To heal this part of myself and move on, I had to get over my self-judgment and focus on my self-worth.

Bad boys act like they're just not that into you because they're not. So, when that mofo tells you he's not serious about you and isn't ready to settle down…believe him.

And if you can't handle having a strictly safe and sexual relationship with him, then don't.

Because they will never say "I'm not having sex with you because I'm not ready for anything serious" now do they?

He seems exciting because he has nothing to

lose. There is a level of reckless abandon with someone who has nothing to abandon.

He doesn't have a job to lose, money to lose, shelter to lose nor dignity to lose. He's temporary fun and real life restarts in the morning.

And if he's living with you, at some point, you're going to want him to pay some bills.

That stellar sex appeal? Blame your ovaries for that.

Studies show that our inner lady parts RESPOND to bad boys because THEY (ovaries) think he'd be good for procreation and sticking around.

What a joke, right?

I tend to believe in science, but I kind of hope this isn't true. I hope this was one of those inconclusive case studies because how could our own bodies betray us like this?

Experience showed me that although he may be hypnotizing now, he'll be horrendous later. I saw it with my own eyes, so I believe it.

He's a master manipulator who weaponizes his nonchalance because the more he pulls away the harder you try for his attention.

He's dangling a carrot like you're a horse in training.

He's a sporadic communicator, you can't

confront him about anything, and he only shows 'affection' when he's horny and you're the easiest to "horn dog" on.

So, when he texts "wyd" after nine days you feel validated because "aww, he thought about me."

He really wants to know what you're doing late at night so that he can come through for his inconsistent booty call because no one else is available or willing at the time.

A bad boy's sex is supposed to be magnificent, but women's orgasm rates beg to differ.

Embarrassingly, I've heard of many women citing dickmatization as the reason they accept trash ass behavior. The dick is supposed to be so good that they can't break away.

I just roll my eyes because this is not a thing.

Women hardly ever have orgasms through penetration; it's like 8% who do. Tell me, what does that tell you?

You're letting a male who thinks your period comes out of your ass, can't find the clitoris, and gives you a partial hysterectomy with his tongue...use you.

I just want us to do better.

Yes, he's attractive and well-groomed. This is all by design. He's too vain to be raggedy or funky because he is always on the prowl and must look the part.

Because we are sometimes selectively stupid, we equate arrogance to confidence. He feels like he's such a catch, so you do too; he is now in your head.

Males know that a lot of women gravitate to bad boys. They watch TV and listen to rap music too.

And they will wear any costume to get what they want, which is usually sex. For them to believe in their gender superiority, they are ruled by their genitals.

There's been research that shows that men with sociopathic & psychopathic tendencies get the most dates. This is scary.

But it's still not your fault. All this tells me is that males study how to infiltrate and destroy women.

Society has perpetuated this level of misogynistic mayhem and patriarchal pandemonium.

Do not let a certain type of male come into your life and disrupt everything you've worked hard for.

The point of this chapter is to mind your genitals. This means don't lose your brain over temporary ass.

Thoughts...

_____
_____
_____
_____
_____
_____
_____
_____
_____
_____
_____
_____
_____
_____
_____
_____
_____
_____
_____
_____
_____
_____
_____

Chapter Six

RELATIONSHIT R&R: THE "RUNAWAY RULES"

Have you ever reminisced on relationships past and thought, "I waited way too long to get that mofo out of my life?"

This was me too until I learned how to use my safety parachute BEFORE the plane crashed and burned.

I used to be so hard on myself wondering why the hell I waited for things to get to the point of no return before I decided to cut that bitch off.

Sometimes it's hard to figure out if you should leave or stay. Especially if you've never seen a healthy relationship or never been in one.

Add to that, how the patriarchy and fairy tales teach girls and women that if we suffer for love, we will be chosen by Mr. Right in the end.

What they don't tell you is that Mr. Right does not exist because it's impossible for them to escape the misogynistic spectrum altogether.

As women, we even have to undo the "pickme-ism" and male worship that we've internalized just by living in a penis privileged world.

But back to the issue at hand; if you're feeling this "go or stay" confusion then you should probably go. As a matter of fact, go whenever you feel like it.

I don't care if you wake up out of the blue and he's done nothing wrong. If you want to go, then GO.

Most folks break up over cheating, sex, or money. But you have every right to just change your mind about a person. You don't need a reason to bounce.

Women are also taught to stay if you're not being cheated on or hit. Hell, sometimes we're told to stay even if we are being cheated on or hit.

If I'm not happy, I'm leaving no matter how 'normal' the relationship is.

I wasn't always this callous, but I also didn't know any better. Males will play in your face and behind your back. They do what's best for them with no consideration for how you feel.

They will never give you what you crave but will turn around and give the next woman everything you didn't get, plus some.

That's why you need to stop caring about their feelings. He doesn't care when he hurts your feelings by making you feel like you're crazy and didn't see what you saw or hear what you heard (gaslighting).

He doesn't care about your feelings when he's sometimes into you and sometimes not, causing you to try harder and harder for his dusty ass validation (going hot then cold).

He doesn't care about your feelings when he overwhelms you with kind words and gifts, then as soon as you let your guard down, he goes back to his old ways (love bombing).

These emotionally unavailable cretins use these tactics when they feel you are on the verge of finally moving on.

You just have to be strong enough to cry it out and let it burn. The pain will pass. I promise.

Stop reminiscing on all the good times you had. How you used to talk until 3am sacrificing your beauty sleep. How you used to spend your free time together doing absolutely nothing and still have fun.

How he was so funny and made you laugh until you cried.

When most of your good memories are blasts

from the past, it's time to go.

Now, you have nothing to say to him on the phone except, "I'm tired," because you refuse to lose sleep just to hold the phone.

You remind him that your bedtime is in eight minutes because you'd rather clean baseboards than spend time with him.

Now, he has a mean streak and says and does things to hurt you on purpose, or to let you know who's the boss. It's him, he's the boss, by the way.

You cry at night, quietly soaking your pillow, in anguish about whether to break up or stay together.

You've left him more than once, but he always says and does the "right" things to draw you back in.

So, you went back…

But lo and behold, he manipulates the relationship back to his baseline of comfort. And the emotional roller coaster starts all over again.

Once he's back in, he expects you to stop being so sensitive, to NOT talk about your feelings, never challenge that his words and actions don't match, and to NOT use words like "accountability" and "compatibility."

Because if you would just stop being so

dramatic (talking about how you feel) and try things a different way (his way) then you would get along just fine.

This is him trying to brainwash you so that you won't expect to be treated as a person of value.

There is a subset of males who make a living from degrading women. They could never be successful at anything else.

It's you who needs to change if you expect him to stick around and continue blessing you with his less-than-average community peen.

It's you who needs to go to the gym (even though he's the one pregnant) or get more friends so that you won't be all up in his business trying to hold him accountable.

When you finally start realizing that you're not "compatible" it pisses him off because he feels like you just might be waking up from this relationship coma.

As long as you play the game his way, y'all are more than compatible...you're perfect together in his lying eyes.

I had an ex who would spend entire weekends at his friend's version of the playboy mansion versus spending any quality time with me.

I kid you not, whenever we were at my place, he was on his phone 99% of the time and whenever I was at his place, he was on his video game 100% of the time.

However, he had all the time in the world (at least weekends) to be around scantily clad women who lived a no-strings-attached life.

Make no mistake, there will be no women slandered here.

They were just about getting their coins, which I respect. I will never blame another woman for a male's lies and deceit. It is not up to other women to keep a male honest.

If he betrays you, it's his fault. If he cheats on you, it's his fault. Another woman is not responsible for a male's behavior.

What pissed me off is an uneducated, barely literate male insulting my intelligence.

He told me that he was helping to promote these parties and doubling as security to boot. Promotion? Security? Sir, these are activities that one gets paid for and I see no evidence of money.

But what did I do? I justified his actions to myself and hid them from everyone else.

Why? Because I was hurt, embarrassed, and felt stupid.

I told myself that he was different, and we were solid, and that he wouldn't do anything to jeopardize my trust.

Well, he did jeopardize my trust. Surprise,

surprise there, right? And he also had the audacity to be emotionally abusive.

I couldn't express myself to him. He literally would not talk to me about things I needed to talk about to feel better. He would shut down, hang up the phone or deploy a "007 James Bond" diversion tactic.

This diversion usually included blaming me for everything, gaslighting me and calling me crazy or dramatic. He said I was throwing things out of proportion and that the things I cared about were not worth caring about.

So, I learned to eat my feelings which led to sadness and resentment. It also caused me to withdraw and become emotionally distant myself. That's what emotionally abusive relationships do.

He really needed anger management. He would scream, curse, and insult me by playing on what he thought were my insecurities. He would throw up things I'd shared with him when we were in the honeymoon stage of the relationship.

No matter what communication strategy I tried, what relationship quiz I took, or what book I read for advice, he wouldn't listen, change, or apologize.

Now don't get it twisted, I can give just as good as I get, but I didn't want to play tit for tat.

My mouth can be reckless, and I can tear a person limb from limb with the power of my tongue. But I didn't want to have to do this.

One day, I realized that he thrived off the drama, so I decided to cut off his supply. I realized this because even when I would let him "win" the argument he would still go on and on and on.

I realized that he liked the fight.

I would deal with the boredom and unhappiness until I couldn't deal anymore, or until he did something like be inappropriate online. It got to the point that I was hoping for something to break up about.

Then I'd blow up and call it quits. Go no contact. And let the pain burn like that Usher Raymond song. I'd finally start to see the rose-gold lining of the blingy rainbow. Then I'd get the call.

You know the call when he knows you're moving on, and barely think about him anymore, so he "finds" your number?

You get anxious and start hyperventilating because your body is screaming "NO, DON'T ANSWER IT!"

But you answer anyway.

Because you still haven't had enough yet. And

maybe you're not 100% over the relationship.

Eventually he starts making the same promises of change. You eat it all up like it's a steaming bowl of the cheesiest macaroni.

You think you've finally got some common ground: he expects red-district-type acrobatics in the bedroom, and you expect your emotional needs to be met.

You agree to give it one more try, and shortly, thereafter, you realize you've been duped AGAIN.

You've been granting his sexual wishes, and he still doesn't give one damn about your emotional ones.

It was during this cycle of insanity that I learned how to bolt the door and lock the windows to make sure he had no way in ever again.

It was also during this cycle of insanity that I realized I didn't even like him and hadn't for a long time.

I mean, our life values were incongruent at best.

I believe in showing little boys love and affection so that they don't grow up to be sociopaths. He believed in punching lil boys in the chest to make them tough. You know to turn them into men and make their facial hair grow in faster.

We obviously couldn't raise sons together.

I believe that little girls should be affirmed and protected. He thought it was okay to send girls out at night to take out the trash…by herself.

We obviously couldn't raise daughters together.

In my experience, beliefs are usually where that toxic masculinity shows itself in relationships.

If I was still in any of my past mistakes, I wouldn't be able to do what I'm doing right now, which is writing about toxic relationships, helping women recognize red flags and helping women detach from women-hating males.

Life would have still been getting sucked out of me.

I would have been too busy trying to unravel these clues myself. I'd still be in denial myself. I would still be hesitant to ruffle their sensitive feathers, to prevent a fight of epic proportions.

Your growth is stifled when you are in these unhealthy relationships.

You can bet your bottom dollar on that.

It's okay to admit that you don't even like him anymore. You don't like how he talks about women. You don't like that he dresses like a prison inmate. You don't like how belligerent and embarrassing he is in public. You don't like to be around him much at all anymore.

Let's be honest, you settled in the first place. It's okay to think you are better when you are. It's okay to say it too. We are taught to be humble, meek, and grateful for male attention.

I say keeping their attention off you is a lot safer.

So what if you've been together for years. It's happiness over history over here.

So what if you have to learn someone new. You may realize that you want to learn a new hobby versus a new male. Hobbies are more fulfilling anyway.

So what if you have children together. Kids deserve a happy mama.

It's okay to outgrow him. It's okay to realize your own worth. It's okay to want to have a different experience.

It's okay that this type of male no longer suits you.

I had an ex tell me that he didn't have any issues to work on, and he really believed this. I, on the other hand, was dumbfounded.

And this was AFTER he'd given me the list of things he thought I needed to change.

He had major league blind spots for himself, but he could see everyone else's flaws. He

73

even made some up.

It was this relationship that exposed me to trauma bonding, gaslighting and a narcissistic personality.

These types refuse to do the work to heal and evolve.

Therefore, make choices with YOUR best interests in mind.

Sometimes that means being okay with DYING single.

Thoughts...

DUSTY DUDE CHECKLIST

☐	**Vinny the Victim**
☐	Vinny is a deranged mitch who is always crying (sometimes even literally) about how hard his life is even though it's because of his own bad decisions. His favorite song is "oh woe is me," and he thrives on your pity.
☐	Vinny has a lot of kids by a lot of women but doesn't take care of any because he "just ain't got it." And being the victim that he is, the moms are all tripping. After all, how is he supposed to be responsible for his own reproductive organs?!
☐	Vinny guilts you into sticking around to "figure out what's wrong with him." Vincent refuses to understand that you're not a therapist or a castrator. You just want to give up on him too. Oh, Vinny.

☐	**Terry the Toddler**
☐	Terry is the "oh I'ma show you" dude. He purposely does and says things to hurt you because "you gone learn today" not to cross him. Perry acts like a toddler having a tantrum and loves playing tit for tat.
☐	Terry lets fights go on for too long because he loves the intensity and drama. This is another one of Terry's tantrum tactics. He wants his attention any way he can get it, even if it is negative attention.
☐	If you dare to call Terry out for his behavior, he will throw a whole mitch fit. He will point fingers, shift blame, refuse to compromise, take no responsibility and put you in time out (silent treatment).
☐	**Lenny the Lazy**
☐	Lenny doesn't do shit except maybe online game tournaments. He's always lived off a woman and his mother's door revolve for him.

☐	Lenny doesn't understand why he should pay bills because before he moved in you were paying them just fine. He sees no problem here.
☐	For some reason, Lenny is always tired. In addition to providing no financial help, he also doesn't cook or clean. Hell, he's even too lazy to converse coherently.
☐	**Franky the Faker**
☐	Maybe Franky speaks French and is going to take you to Paris because he goes every year you know. And maybe Franky's is full of shit. Franky is a poser, a charlatan and a con artist. And he's not that good at any of these.
☐	Franky tells these elaborate stories about his house, his car and his lucrative job. But in reality, Franky is a delusional unemployed pothead who's car got "repo'd" a few months ago.

☐	Franky is always "coming into a lot of money" and at that time he will be able to purchase his own chicken dinners. But alas, that day never comes. As a matter of fact, Franky owes you some money.
☐	**Sammy the Sociopath**
☐	Sammy is a pathological liar who talks too much. He switches between extreme charm and extreme threats to get what he wants. Sammy's excessiveness is just a cover for his heinous behavior.
☐	Sammy has no compassion or empathy for you. He often takes advantage when you are in a vulnerable or sympathetic situation versus supporting you through it.
☐	Sammy is always right and rarely apologizes, unless it will make him look good. Sammy feels justified in treating you bad, and sometimes it feels like he enjoys your suffering. It's because he does.

Chapter Seven

MAKE UP TO BREAK UP CYCLONE

L et's talk about the reasons you may ignore signs of a toxic ass not-so-merry-go-round relationship.

You are fabulous and feisty and stand up for yourself, which makes you feel vindicated even though he just annihilated your boundaries.

You are addicted to the "break-up to make-up cyclone" and ignore the fact that "on and off" relationships are unstable and unhealthy.

I call it a cyclone because you suffer through a devastating storm every time you go back.

Just like when a lightbulb flickers off and on, you know it's about to go out for good. It's the same with on-again and off-again relationships. It's not going to work.

Just because you're assertive and outspoken

doesn't mean you're not in an abusive relationship. As a matter of fact, there is a subset of human males whose main goal is to take a strong woman down to the depths of hell to prove to himself that he can break her.

I LOVE being a feisty firecracker, but not when I have to weaponize it. I got tired of saying "all my life I had to fight!" Ain't you tired now?

When you have to fuss, cuss, or physically fight with someone, you are not in a healthy relationship, no matter how much you fuss, cuss, or fight back.

Yes, you'll have disagreements, But HOW you fight and HOW you resolve things is the difference between a healthy or unhealthy relationship.

I'm about as feisty as they come because I had to overcome so much fear and victimization as a kid. I identified so much with Oz's the cowardly lion because I was too afraid to stand up for myself inside and outside the home.

So, when I "got grown," I told myself that I would say what I needed to say, and do what I needed to do, to NOT be taken advantage of. I would do whatever it takes to protect myself.

My feistiness looks like out-witting you with my intelligence and using my tongue as a sword. And baby it's double-edged! You betta ask somebody.

I'm also street smart from how I grew up, so I can curse like a sailor and put together magnificent profane combinations. In other words, I can give it to you however you want it.

But being quick-witted and sharp-tongued has no effect in abusive relationships. Your abuser will use your defense as fuel for their hellfire.

Males who love drama and chaos and will beat you at this "game" with experience. He'll tell you that he hates drama and can't stand it, but his actions will prove that he really lives for it.

As far as physical abuse, have the police escort an abusive mofo out of your vicinity. And let the chips fall where they may. You have no business going toe-to-toe with a penis person.

In the previous chapter we talked about dating down.

Now, we're talking about dating dumb.

I "dated dumb" by telling myself that at least I didn't take his shit, which was exactly what I was doing by not leaving.

I also realized that my alter ego "Lil Feisty" was keeping me in denial. In my mind, things weren't so bad since I was tough enough to dish out some nastiness of my own.

Eventually, I realized that I didn't want to be

THAT girl.

That girl who:

is always cussing her man out because she found out he was cheating...again

is always fussing because her man keeps "borrowing" money...and never paying it back

is always arguing because her relationship thrived off the drama

has to put up the fisticuffs with a man whose physical strength quadruples hers

Which brings me to my next very apropos point.

Lots of women don't realize they are in abusive relationships when there is no physical abuse involved.

Therefore, we are about to discuss the other abuses that should also be deal breakers.

Mental abuse is you being told that you are always wrong or stupid, which is why he needs to make all the decisions for both of you.

These decisions may range from how you dress to how often you can see your family or friends. If you try thinking for yourself, he will go all out to make you doubt yourself.

He will provoke and harass you to anger, then blame you for finally blowing up. He will not give up on his agenda until you are agreeing with his views or are too weary (from fighting) to decide.

He will use these kinds of words to describe you: weak, sensitive, overreacting, confused, stupid, and emotional.

Emotional abuse is when you are constantly being criticized, your feelings and opinions are never valued, and you are treated maliciously until you give up or give in to what he wants.

Emotional abuse is the sibling of mental abuse. Where there is one there is usually the other.

He does and says things that he knows will hurt you but calls you "crazy" or "out of control" if you strike back. His intentions are to mold you like clay into an isolated and fearful woman.

His control issues (disguised as "helping you") cause you to feel depressed, confused, and unstable.

You are constantly crying and walking on eggshells to "keep the peace." Your daily actions depend on his mood of the day.

Verbal Abuse is when words are used as weapons to abuse you.

This includes insults, name-calling, screaming, cursing, threats and harassment.

He'll provoke you into being "feisty" and giving as good as you get so that he can say "see you're abusive too."

This is manipulative mind games, by the way. When you fight back because you feel at risk, it is self-defense NOT mutual abuse.

You are trying to re-establish your independence in the relationship...NOT control him. Thus, no abuse.

But he will use your emotional stress to confuse you and make you feel bad, which gives him the upper hand.

That's why it's important to know the signs and not play the game.

Financial abuse is when he restricts your access to money and/or steals your money.

Did you know that financial abuse is often the first sign of dating violence and domestic abuse?

Or that 99% of domestic violence cases also involve financial abuse?

Financial abuse diminishes your capacity to support yourself because you are unable to acquire, use and maintain financial resources.

That's why I always tell women to HAVE YOUR OWN MONEY, even if you do have a male who provides financially.

Women are financially independent now more than ever in history. This is why you've seen more and more males diminishing our education and high-earning careers.

They know that knowledge is power, and that money is necessary and makes life easier.

They don't want us to have the type of security that we have provided for ourselves.

If we are unable to support ourselves, like our foremothers were, they will be in a place of power over us again.

We would have to settle for their abuse, mediocrity, and lack of likeability to survive. For this reason, let's go deeper into what financial abuse looks like.

Examples of financial abuse:

feeling entitled to your money or assets (even opening your bank statements and other financial records)

borrowing money or making charges without paying (over drafted accounts and maxed out credit cards)

making you account for every penny you spend, forcing you to pay for his bills, because he's already spent his money for personal gain

using your money for his benefit without asking

not allowing you to spend money on yourself (hair, nails, clothes, hobbies…etc.)

confiscating your paycheck or other income

demanding you bail him out of difficult financial situations

interfering with your job or not allowing you to work

Okay, it's time for my "I once had an ex" story that involved financial abuse. I cringe to tell it, but I feel like full transparency is needed here.

So…I once had an ex (sigh) who sold my car without my consent. I know, I was just as shocked as you are when I found out!

Let me backup so that you can understand why I didn't know immediately.

The car no longer worked, and he was supposed to be helping me get it fixed. He told me he'd had it taken to a mechanic he knows. But in reality, he had taken it to the junkyard and sold it for parts.

I found out by mistake, y'all!

A mutual friend who did not know that "EX-broke-bitch" had lied to me, casually mentioned the tyrannical transaction.

I don't know how much he got for parts from MY CAR, and I never saw a penny of that money. I should have had him prosecuted, but instead I had his broke down heap of metal towed from my yard.

It wasn't the same as selling it, but he had to come up off some money to get his own car back. I only hope that it was the same amount, or more, that he got for selling mine.

Unfortunately, we can get addicted to the break-up to make-up cyclone. Most of us have been there. You break up, he apologizes, you take him back, his behavior doesn't change, you break up, he apologizes, you take him back, his behavior doesn't change, you break up, he apologizes, you take him back, his behavior doesn't change…

You get the point.

Now, let's talk about why you get addicted to this cyclone. The intensity of the chase gives you a temporary high. During his apology phase, he's the attentive male he was when you first met, and this gives you false hope that things can go back to the way they were.

But this will never happen because no real work to change has been done. If it's one cliché that I bank on, it's that "talk is cheap."

Another reason you get addicted is because when intensity is based around betrayal, drama, and passionate reconciliations (like make-up sex), it creates a trauma bond.

Trauma bonds are psychological responses to abuse. They form through a cyclone of abuse that is enforced through rewards and punishments.

Here's an example of how trauma bonds form:

The betrayal - he cheated (again)

The drama - you cry, scream, curse and tell him to go to hell (or at least to his mom's)

The passion - he wipes your tears, begs for forgiveness, promises to never to do it again and you have make-up sex (the best it's been in months)

For a while you go on dinner dates or shopping sprees or to see chick flicks. Or whatever activity that he never partakes in unless y'all are in the reconciliation stage.

You buy into his story because you want so bad for it to be different this time. Despite the facts that are glaring at you like neon flashers.

You forgive him (again) versus waiting to see actual change that never happens (again).

The cycle continues…

Here's the problem: you are confusing intensity with intimacy. They are not the same. One is destructive to a relationship and the other is like aloe vera to a relationship.

You know when you have aloe vera because it's soothing.

Soothing to me is having an emotional maturity, trust with secrets, healthy coexisting, reaching goals together, safety, security, and provision.

I value relationships with fair fighting,

meaning no hitting below the belt. Where you both maintain a sense of understanding for each other's needs.

I want someone who is more concerned with harmony in the relationship versus "winning" an argument.

Before I walk on eggshells to not "rub a male the wrong way" or "step on his toes," he'll have to go argue with his mammy.

I protect my peace of mind like my sanity depends on it. Because it does.

Nothing destroys trust like an inconsistent ass male. If he's using his time and attention like a yo-yo, then you need to pack up your pussy and go. You don't have time for a male who blows hot and then cold.

Those are mind games to keep you in your place and train you on what to expect or not expect from him.

If I'm with a male, you best believe that he applied major pressure. Gone are the days where I would convince myself that the bare minimum was enough. You got to be solid in your feelings and intentions for me.

The best way to deal with these types is to never deal with them in the first place. I said the best way to deal with these types is to never deal with them in the first place.

But we all know that these "types" are dealt

with all too often.

There are ways to avoid these trash-bag-ass relationships but be WILLING to die single because MOST males are unworthy of you. I'm just keeping it real.

You avoid them by knowing what red flags to look out for. Then you burn those flags like I want to burn all bras.

Then you have to take action. This means that when you see the flags waving, stop pretending that the carnival is in town.

Admit that it's a danger zone, put on your hazmat suit, and evacuate immediately.

Granted, you can't always tell if you're getting involved with a lunatic because they hide it very well at first. BUT there are usually some kinks in their carefully constructed armor that you can spot if you have the right knowledge.

A major kink is him being controlling. This typically comes into play a little at a time. It may be so subtle at first that it might not even register.

For instance, he may offer to help with your budget as a cover for gaining access to your finances. Never give out your banking passwords, account passwords, account numbers, investment information or other financial records.

This is a gateway to financial abuse.

I don't give a fuck what he says he needs it for. Always protect your money! I am a strong advocate AGAINST couples having joint accounts. The exception is a brand-new SEPARATE account that you put housing expenses into. If he provides financially 100%, then you don't even need to do that.

Another subtle control technique is isolating you from your family and friends. This will be minimal at first, so you don't realize what's going on.

He'll tell you your parents, sister or best friend don't really like him, so that in your loyalty to him, you stop going around them too.

If you try to laugh it off, he'll say they gave him a dirty look behind your back or mumbled something about him under their breath (that you conveniently didn't hear).

Just like the last time he told the truth...this never happened.

Pay close attention out in these streets. Don't delude yourself into staying in a toxic situation because you think you can handle it.

There are males who have dedicated their entire lives to using and abusing women.

Thoughts...

Chapter Eight

DAMSEL IN ~~DISTRESS~~ DEFENSE

I once had an ex get mad, throw a kid-fit and mans-plain to me because I didn't want to listen to the misogynistic gangster rapper he was blasting from his car.

Mind you, we were supposedly on a "date," so I was just not there for it.

Now, I love a good beat sometimes myself and I know that as women we don't always listen to the words that culture destroyers say.

For the most part, I let folks "do them," but since this was supposed to be a mutually enjoyable moment, I said what I said.

Which was "can we please listen to something else?"

Instead of finding a mutually pleasant sound for our ears, he decided to weaponize my feelings.

Apparently, I was supposed to be immune to the disrespect that the mumble rapper was spewing because the lyrics didn't literally pertain to our relationship.

Well, that's up for debate, but even if it were true, that still wasn't the point.

So, being the great debater that I am, I wanted to know HOW it didn't pertain to us since he was advocating for the mindset and language that turns me off.

He thought I was being nonsensical (my word) and pro-woman (his word), which in his brain equated to the same thing.

I'm definitely pro-woman, so I was actually thinking that this was the last time I'd ever deal with a male who thinks that misogyny and patriarchal abuse are their birthright.

There was nothing he could say that was going to shut me up on why I didn't want to hear about how big a man's penis is and how it's the greatest gift to his "bitches and hoes."

I was not letting him use his inept practice of reverse psychology on me that day and he was big mad.

This male-child was trying to gaslight me so that I would think it was something wrong with me for NOT wanting to hear about the degradation of women.

Mind you, he listened to his preferred music choices all the time. So, my not wanting to hear it during what was supposed to be my time should not have been a problem.

Hell, we could have simply talked for that matter. Anything but this.

And I still don't think I was being unreasonable. Middle finger to whomever thinks I was.

Back to gaslighting. It's a diversion tactic to keep you confused and emotionally off balance.

This tactic is used to manipulate you into thinking you are being overly dramatic, or at the least, misunderstanding what's staring you right in the face.

To him I was missing the point, which was that this type of music was simply entertainment to him. And he insinuated that I was being simple-minded by being offended by his entertainment.

Then he started man-splaining.

"All rapper dude was trying to say is that he's out in these streets grinding (selling drugs) and when he gets home, he just wants his property (woman of the night) to cater to his sexual needs because he deserves it."

Huh?

Conversations like this show you where a

man's mental capacity is. It also shows you his level of emotional intelligence.

Males like this refuse to see your point of view and insist on misunderstanding you.

Why? Because they perpetuate macro-aggressions and disrespect toward women any chance they get.

Since he didn't understand, I explained it to him. The lyrics were grating on my nerves like Styrofoam being rubbed together, and killing my vibe, like a party with no birthday.

I went on to say that I did not want to hear about this rapper's penile appendage regardless of how big, how good, or how comatose it fictitiously made women.

As a matter of fact, I was entering a coma myself because ignorance was not being as blissful as people say it is.

I also didn't want to hear women being called bitches, hoes, or gold diggers for gold that we all know doesn't exist.

Do you know what imbecilic thing he had the nerve to say to me?

He said, "you just don't respect men." I almost got whiplash turning around to see if he was serious. Despite my delusional hopes, he was not joking.

Now, I don't respect males in general, but this

wasn't a time that I was exhibiting this.

To him, since I was so eloquently arguing my points, I was being disrespectful. What he meant was that I wouldn't shut up and let him be right about me.

Males use stupidity like hot lava in an attempt to incinerate our brain cells. They embrace misogyny and sexism, then degrade women for speaking out against it.

They believe that the patriarchy reigns supreme and that women are less valuable than them. This is why I don't respect them.

They also believe that women should be barefoot and pregnant, stupidly submissive and expect to be groped depending on their wardrobe choice of the day.

This is why I don't respect them.

They pretend to be traditional until it's time to pay all the bills. Then they want to know what you bring to the table, also known as, how much money you make.

They continue to perpetuate ideals that women should be the sole cooks, cleaners and caretakers to the kids. And let's not forget, wash his drawers, and fix his plate. But make sure it's a glass plate. No paper plates allowed.

This is why I don't respect them.

They want to be leaders with no leadership

qualities. True leaders are out there building, protecting, and providing. Not arguing over hip hop and paper plates.

This is why I don't respect them.

If you speak up for yourself, he may scream, insult you or try to convince you that you are the problem.

What he really means is that you need to shut the fuck up and stay in a woman's place. And your place is NOT to be standing up to him or to have your own opinions.

Remind them that your place is at the top.

They will tell you out of their own uncouth mouths that men are superior to women. It doesn't matter that you are smarter, have more money and show empathy toward others.

This is what society has brainwashed us all with, but unlike you and I, he is incapable of thinking in new ways. He truly believes that having a penis and bicep strength makes him superior.

He suffers from high self-esteem with no justifiable proof to support his arrogance. There's no cure for him.

He doesn't get along with any women. He'll beef with his mother, aunt, daughter, wife, girlfriend, his friend's girlfriend, and his granny if she "gets out of line."

He sees compromising with women as bowing down to them and that is unacceptable to him.

He's simple-minded enough to think that if he doesn't call you out of your name out loud, then he is respecting you.

By his logic, cheating isn't real if you don't catch him naked, conjoined and in bed with someone.

If you don't have a preponderance of the evidence, he will play his mind games until you give up the fight and apologize to him for your outrageous accusations.

Let him go play with his mama.

These types believe that ALL women are desperate to have a husband, so he uses this as ammo against you. He may mention your age and how you'd better snag your husband before it's too late.

He may make fun of your weight by buying you a waist trainer even though he looks like he's 13 months preggers.

He expects and demands blind loyalty from you while he's messaging Instagram models while you're asleep.

He will compare you to other women to point out how inferior you are. Or compare you to his exes who were smart enough to leave him.

He'll make fun of women he thinks are

unattractive and sneakily take pictures of them to share on his social media for the laughs and giggles of his fellow losers.

Speaking of social media, his is full of offensive material to women. So much so, that you don't even follow him because his memes make you cringe and grit your teeth.

Males with this mindset spew that ignorant nonsense that all problems in the home, and in the community, are the fault of women.

It's not the male's fault because he didn't stick around to make a difference one way or the other. I've literally heard this used as justification for a male abandoning his family.

This is why I don't respect them.

If by chance something traumatic happens in his life where he is forced to change, it will NOT be because you were the long-suffering damsel by his side.

He's not going to change for you.

It's up to YOU to change so that you have a better chance of avoiding dust antics altogether.

Stop making assumptions about what he is thinking. Stop ignoring his behavior and call him out on his disrespect. Stop making excuses about what he is saying.

He is showing you who he is so believe him.

There are too many women who think that they are strong enough to deal with a male's dysfunction until he is ready to change.

However, because you have the capacity to, doesn't mean that you should.

What about you? What is this relationship costing you?

I'll tell you what it's costing…it's costing too much.

Let's talk about accountability.

One of the biggest mistakes you can make is procreating with males like these. Do not be reckless with your womb.

I know that they lie and deceive to get the women they want, and sometimes you find out after the deed is done.

They love to shout about women trying to trap them with babies. But many a male have weaponized their sperm to sabotage and control women.

My hope is that this book cuts back some on your learning curve. A lot of what I cover was never taught to me. I had to learn everything I know about abusive relationships the hard way.

I don't want that for you.

If you want to get married, make sure you protect your assets. Marriage was created to oppress women in that it gave males ownership over their wives.

Who, pray tell, needs to be owned?

Today's woman is financially independent and has more rights. Use these to your advantage and not to your detriment.

If you must get married, marry a male who sees you as his equal, and SHOWS it too.

I believe in women having EVERYTHING they desire. Just be smart about it.

Be a damsel in defense of your money, your sanity, and your edges.

Thoughts...

Chapter Nine

BLACK FEMICIDE & INTIMATE PARTNER VIOLENCE (IPV)

Those who gatekeep the dysfunction in the black community aren't going to like this chapter.

But as I've said in other chapters, I don't give a fuck.

The days of black male worship must end for the self-preservation of black girls and women.

I said what I said.

Femicide, as defined by the World Health Organization (WHO), is the intentional murder of women because they are women, but broader definitions include killings of women or girls.

FBI estimates that four black females were killed each day in 2020. (2021)

The FBI and CDC found that Black girls and

women were the most often killed among female demographics last year. (October 2021)

If racism were to end today, black girls and women would still be in trouble. Because the people who hurt and kill us the most, look like us.

I'm speaking about the black male.

When I walk out of my door every morning, it is not the white male that I'm afraid of.

And with stats and facts like the ones above, who could blame me?

I think of the four black women who will be killed today for trying to leave an abusive and controlling black male.

And I'll go to the platforms of those who share the faces and names of "today's four" with a sense of dread and anxiety.

Dread because I KNOW the four will be there. Anxiety because it's traumatic feeling like prey every day.

And nobody seems to care except for a few women who are brave enough to call out this epidemic in the black community.

Not the black women politicians we have elected. Not the elected officials at the national level. Certainly not the pickmes and mammies who protect black male degeneracy.

But what about the white male, you ask?

Of course, I've felt the ramifications of racism.

However, I feel the effects of sexism and gender-based violence much more.

I feel the heaviness of black femicide every day. Some days I can't even look at "today's four."

Four black females per day.

Every six hours.

Where does this hatred of black girls and women stem from?

I believe it stems from being at the bottom in desirability, education, and employability due to their criminal histories.

And of course, they blame black women like we have somehow sold them out when really all we did was capitalize on opportunities.

They are angry because they are expected to provide. But the provision no longer comes with the power to abuse.

Because women can earn their own money now.

They know that money gives us options and freedoms, and that is exactly what they don't want us to have.

The option to choose a suitable and likable partner.

The freedom to walk away any time we want

to.

We no longer have to accept struggle love or mediocre provisions. We are now able to take care of ourselves.

They NEED someone to be beneath them.

You see, oppression is the language of males. You can look in any corner of the Earth to see this.

More than four in ten Black women experience physical violence from an intimate partner during their lifetimes. White women, Latinas, and Asian/Pacific Islander women report lower rates.

Black women also experience significantly higher rates of psychological abuse — including humiliation, insults, name-calling, and coercive control — than do women overall.

Sexual violence affects Black women at high rates. More than 20 percent of Black women are raped during their lifetimes — a higher share than among women overall.

Black women face a particularly high risk of being killed at the hands of a man. A 2015 Violence Policy Center study finds that Black women were two and a half times more likely to be murdered by men than their White counterparts. More than nine in ten Black female victims knew their killers.

Many of our foremothers didn't remarry after their husbands abandoned them or died, because they were happy to be free from their oppressor.

They try to coerce submission because they want blind loyalty, and even blinder sacrifice.

They are all over social media blaming welfare, makeup, hair weaves, feminism, and the white man for their shortcomings.

But they won't address their lack of education, lack of desirability and being unemployable due to their criminal histories.

However, when the truth is being told, like now, we are called bitter and overly emotional.

They cannot understand how we still thrive, shine, live well, and get the bag with so much hatred aimed toward us.

It's because we've had to. We've had to be smart, resourceful, resilient, and creative enough to outmaneuver intersectionality (being black AND female).

Until black males start holding each other accountable for sexual deviance and black femicide rates it will be 'all black males' to me.

There are two legal loopholes that leave domestic violence victims and survivors unprotected:

The Boyfriend Loophole

Federal law prohibits domestic abusers from having guns, but only if they have been married to, have lived with, or have a child with the victim. It does not otherwise prohibit abusive dating partners from having guns. This gap in the law is known as the "boyfriend loophole" and has become increasingly deadly. The share of homicides committed by dating partners has been increasing for three decades, and now women are as likely to be killed by dating partners as by spouses.

The Stalker Loophole

If a person is convicted of felony stalking, current federal law only prohibits them from accessing guns, but people convicted of misdemeanor stalking can still legally obtain guns.

The more we divest from males who historically beat, rape and murder girls and women...the more violent they become.

Therefore, it's very important for us to learn how to physically defend ourselves and acquire our "carry concealed weapon" license.

Stop advocating for defunding the police.

Stop marching, looting, and protesting.

Stop voting for politicians who don't care about the black femicide rate in this country.

Stop being race and gender loyal to those who'd rather see you dead.

Save yourself.

Thoughts...

_____

_____

_____

_____

_____

_____

_____

_____

_____

_____

_____

_____

_____

_____

_____

_____

_____

_____

_____

_____

_____

_____

_____

5 STEPS TO QUICKLY HEAL FROM A BREAKUP

Go No Contact:

No contact is MANDATORY if you want to get over a breakup as fast as you can. This means blocking him EVERYWHERE. "No contact" is not to punish your ex. It is for you to have space and time to DETACH. It is also for you to get used to the relationships being OVER.

Write it out:

Write down EVERY NEGATIVE THING he's ever SAID or DONE to you. Write down how his words and actions made you feel. Write down how he reacted to your pain. Write down how he didn't try to fix it. This will help you to stop romanticizing about him.

Talk it out:

If there's someone you can trust and tell the ugly/embarrassing stuff to...call them UP. Purging how you feel is therapeutic. Having someone to listen without judgment is priceless. AND It helps to say things out loud because it reminds you WHY you're DONE.

Cry it out:

Water (your tears) is a healer and a cleanser. Yes, breaking up hurts like hell, BUT the pain is TEMPORARY. There is strength in vulnerability. And if you stick with this process you will reach the other side of sorrow quicker.

He's Dead to You:

It's OK to grieve because something HAS died...your relationship. When someone dies there is NO WAY for reconciliation. And when you think there is, you don't completely let go. He's not dead, but proceed as if he is. DO NOT leave yourself open. His time is up!

FINAL THOUGHTS: YOU BETTER JUDGE THAT BOOK BY ITS COVER

Most women settle.

Here are thirty of the main reasons we do so.

Number One…

You are the self-improvement Queen.

You've excelled in education, finances, and career. You are constantly improving yourself through classes, courses, reading, traveling, or finding new experiences.

You go to therapy when you need to, because you're self-aware enough to know when you have some things to work on.

Therefore, you think you can improve the

117

relationship if you just use what you've learned on him…so you stay.

He seems to get better, even if it's minuscule effort, so you trick yourself into thinking your methods are working. Your hopes are UP and…now you're hooked.

You KNOW deep down that you can only change you, but you SOOO want him to change…so you try harder.

And the cycle continues until you've wasted more months or years on a dead-end relationship that crashes and burns anyway.

You're in the "I stayed, got hooked and tried harder" cycle.

Number Two…

You're scared that your time is running out.

After all, there are marriages to be had and babies to be made, right?

And you "ain't getting no younger" as older folks have a rude way of reminding you.

So even though the "he's the wrong male for me" signs are flashing like hazard lights, you ignore them.

When you make choices out of fear you become more willing to stay in relationships that are no good for you, with males who are no good for you.

On a deeper level, you may be a prisoner to the myth that you have to lock down a male quick, fast or in a hurry to get a ring and a baby.

And if you don't, then you're not doing what women are 'supposed to do,' or what 'real women' do.

You're afraid that your biological clock won't tick or tock.

Number Three...

You Fear Dying Alone

You are intimidated by being alone, but the bigger fear is wasting your precious time with the wrong male.

When you know how to enjoy your own company, and you build an independent and satisfying life, you are in a space that allows you to choose a partner that is worthy of your presence.

When you feel anxious or afraid to be alone, you may have developed a reliance on codependency.

This can lead you to choose the wrong male from a place of desperation, rather than a place of wholeness.

You must be willing to die alone versus settling for trash.

Number Four…

The relationship feels familiar to you.

There is this sense of comfort, and it feels like you've known him forever.

You think this familiarity is a good thing.

As it turns out, you're right, and you're wrong.

You're right that he's familiar because he's the same type of guy that you've been dating over and over.

"Same shit, different toilet," as they say.

You're wrong because this is NOT a good thing.

In this case, familiarity does indeed breed contempt.

Number Five...

You are unconsciously drawn to the same type.

We are often unconsciously drawn to the same dysfunction over and over because we are hard-wired from our childhoods.

Relationship dysfunction is often a symptom of childhood wounds or trauma.

I call these relationships "wave the white flag romances" because we surrender to the dysfunction due to that familiarity I mentioned above.

Studies show that we are often drawn to partners who have the same negative characteristics as our primary caregivers, which are usually our parents or guardians.

It's time to burn the white flags.

Number Six…

You're in denial but yours isn't the river flowing through Egypt.

This means that you are DETERMINED to find the teeniest tiniest change or difference to justify why you are settling for the wrong male.

"I saw him read the cereal box once so that must mean he loves to read."

Because he is slightly (like one billionth of a millimeter) better than your last male, you've gone blind, deaf, and dumb to his shortcomings.

You justify and excuse his bad behavior over and over again, because admitting will mean you have to do something about it.

While your rational mind knows you are engaging in the same unhealthy dating habits, your denial is keeping you looped in...and loopy.

Time to take off those rose-gold-tinted glasses.

Number Seven...

You've never seen a healthy relationship.

So, you don't know what a healthy relationship

dynamic looks like.

And as far as you can see, everyone around here is settling in mediocre and unbalanced unions.

And you think that's just how relationships are supposed to be. This is normal to you.

You don't know what values to look for, what questions to ask and what red flags to watch out for.

Time for a new normal.

Number Eight…

You were neglected or abused as a little girl.

It wasn't until I went to college that I realized not all little black girls grew up like I did.

There were girls who had fathers who adored them and treated them like royalty.

Since they were treated like royalty, they

sought other royals.

These girls grew into women who had very high standards regarding the males they chose.

Because they had positive examples of how they should be treated, they knew what it felt like to be respected and made to feel special.

And like you do; they gravitate to what feels familiar to them.

The unfortunate part is that you didn't learn feel-good relationship tips from your father, or uncles, or male cousins or male friends.

Time to replace the trash with treasure.

Number Nine…

You think the sex is too good to leave.

I got to call you out because this is bullshit. This is a sorry and weak cop-out.

I've never had sex that changed my life.

Never.

Not even once.

I'm willing to bet that you haven't either.

It's another excuse to keep going back. AND you think it's a reason that may garner you some understanding.

I don't understand.

Despite what males may think, their sex organ cannot save the world.

I mean, look around you…there is still flood, famine, and disease across the land.

Stop drinking the "I'm dickmatized" Kool-Aid.

It's NOT a real thing.

Dickmatization does not exist.

Number Ten...

You date for shallow reasons.

He LOOKS like he'd be good in bed. Your mind's telling you "NO", but your ovaries are telling you "Yes."

He's so cute that other women will be jealous.

He must be over six feet tall because 5'11" is just UN-ACCEP-TABLE.

He has an eight pack. I mean, that's TWO EXTRA PACKS.

He smiles too much. The dark, broody, and angry are more your speed.

He wears Cole Haan and not Timberland. You love a man with some swag and street cred.

He's too "nice." I mean, he's never even had to go to anger management!

127

On second thought, these are all acceptable reasons.

Just as males have their preferences, so should you have yours.

In shallow situations, make sure NOT to confuse a good time with trying to turn a hoe into a husband.

Carry on.

Number Eleven…
You love you a fixer upper.

You know exactly who I'm talking about.

He's downtrodden.
He's broken-spirited.
He's broke-in-money.
He's broken down.

But for some reason you think you can transform Mr. Wrong into "Mr. Right for me."

128

He's your pet project.

Your "I think I can."

And dammit if you can't fix him…then maybe you can at least save him.

Ma'am you are not Thomas the Train.

I don't think you can CAN'T enough.

Number Twelve…

You like being Captainess Save a Heaux.

For what though?

What knight on a white steed rode in to save you?

And if he's so fixable, then why hasn't anyone else been able to get the job done?

You google "how to find a good man," but fail

to see how you are complicit in him staying a loser.

When we date males we need to "fix," or find ourselves in a pattern of dating males who bring us down, it's likely that we have some inner healing that needs to be done.

You will never get this healing in a "captainess save a heaux" relationship because he is damaged himself.

He cannot VALIDATE you, nor UPLEVEL your life in any way because HE is more limited than you are.

And believe me when I say he has no burning desire to make your life better.

You can't love away his problems any more than he can "mooch off you" enough to heal your wounds.

Change has to come from within for the both of you.

Let go of the heroine complex.

130

Number Thirteen…

You are addicted to the infatuation phase.

Most relationships start out with an overdose of lust, infatuation, and endorphins (feel-good hormones).

He's just wonderfully magnificent at first, right?

More intriguing than irritating.

More satisfying than stupid.

More desirable than disgusting.

You're all, "his negatives are so petite that I barely notice them."

You're infatuated.

But then the hammer drops because infatuation, by definition, is intense and short-lived.

Those little things you ignored during lust and romance are now irritating as fuck.

Now, you're looking for your next temporary fix.

Let the next fix be YOU.

Number Fourteen...

You allowed him to move you too fast.

Well, it didn't take you long to get here – another failed relationship three months in.

You were so busy moving too fast that the red flags were a blur before you ever noticed them.

You never really got to know him, or his gross hygiene or his anger issues.

You didn't take enough time to investigate his stories that never quite seemed to add up.

Now you can stand for him to touch you

anymore.

And you feel stuck because mr. opportunistic won't go away.

Why would he when he's the one benefiting the most.?

You also don't want to have to recover from another failed relationship.

If he's rushing, then there's a dusty ass reason.

Number Fifteen…

You think he's going to change.

If you are saying to yourself that you can change him, think about what that really means.

Most likely it means he's a repeat offender of breaking your deal-breakers.

And he's smashed your values to bits like a category five hurricane.

Changing takes a lot of maturity, emotional availability, inner work, and sometimes outer work like exercise.

Now ask yourself…

Is he mature, available, self-aware, and as fierce about improving as you are?

If not, chalk your differences up to incompatibility.

And throw him the middle finger AND the deuces at the same damn time.

Accept that he's the wrong male for you.

The only thing you should worry about changing…is your mind about him.

Number Sixteen…

Your potential-partner-picker is broken.

You may be approached by males with impeccable integrity, honorable intentions, successful jobs, and lucrative credit scores.

You know, males on the same level as you. But you won't give him the time of day.

As you turn away from someone who MIGHT be worth a little of your time, you catch the eye of Dusty McMusty.

He's a homebody (aka on house arrest),

He's got that paper (nope, not money…he's ON paper aka parole),

And his hobby is playing any version of GTA (grand theft auto).

Don't give your number to Dusty Mc.

Number Seventeen…

You think he'll be different for you.

So…he hasn't been to any of his kids' birthday parties, school assemblies, field trips, honor celebrations, or just generally hung out with

135

them in years.

He's been too busy with his career (criminally, that is) and broadening his horizons (getting über high).

Do you run for the hills screaming "someone get this beast away from me?"

Nope.

You have your own child by him and think suddenly, he's going to be involved, present and responsible.

Don't breed with them.

Number Eighteen…

You don't realize that he hates women.

Does he badmouth his mom, his aunts, his sisters, his girl cousins, and his many exes for how they have aided in the ruination of his life?

Do most of his coma-inducing diatribes start with "y'all females?"

He has no issue generally bad-mouthing women.

He waxes poetic about the horrible times his "bitch of a mother" hurt him.

He says things like "all hoes be out for money."

Yes, he has baggage and a background (like we all do), but you need to pay attention to his words and his actions.

This type of male has NOT dealt with his issues, and you don't want him dealing with them on you.

He hates women and this includes you.

Number Nineteen…

You don't recognize the danger signs of abuse.

Have you thought more than once that he could benefit from court-appointed anger management?

Does he resolve conflict through violence, threats, screaming and destroying property.

Would his escalation of behavior come off as psychotic in normal society?

Even if he is not using that anger on you, this is not acceptable behavior, and you should run FAST.

Or it will be you soon.

Number Twenty…

You view unacceptable behavior as little blips on the radar.

It is not normal to only hear from a man unless he wants sex, whether it's at 3 PM or 3 AM.

It is not normal to be dating someone, but never meet his friends or family, and never be invited to any gathering with said friends or family.

It is not normal to pay for most (or all) of the food, the rent, utilities, y'all's dates, his clothes, his shoes, or any other of his expenses, wants or needs.

It is also not normal to deal with an imbecile who regularly insults you, embarrasses you, or disrespects you in any shape, form, or fashion.

Even if he was "just kidding."

This non-exhaustive list should NEVER become the norm for you.

It's not a blip, it's betrayal.
Number Twenty-One…

You don't have bonafide deal breakers or strong boundaries.

You should have an open-ended (because you will need to add to it) deal breaker list.

This list should include behaviors you simply won't tolerate. Add to the list above

Figure out which character traits and behaviors you won't accept and stand on your decision.

You should also have a list of values that are important to you that are non-negotiable.

Stop having boundaries that are easier to break than a chicken egg.

Knowing what you want helps you avoid males who possess traits and values that make him wrong for you.

Cheating should not be your only deal breaker.

Number Twenty-Two...

You have low self-esteem.

Nothing demolishes your chances of having an intimate and reciprocal relationship like chronic low self-esteem.

Self-esteem is what you think about yourself, how you feel about yourself and how you let others treat you.

It impacts what you think you deserve and what you will accept.

When you operate from a place of low self-esteem you are more likely to ignore red flags, disregard your boundaries and settle for less.

It's time to deal with your self-sabotaging patterns.

Number Twenty-Three…

You haven't done your own inner work.

The most important step you can take to break your old dating patterns is to do the inner work to deal with your own issues.

For instance, did you have an abusive and narcissistic father? You may have daddy issues you're unaware of.

Have you always felt confused about your purpose in life?

141

You may find yourself attracted to workaholics, or at the other extreme, AGAINST-workaholics.

Did you have a controlling and overbearing mother? You may fall for guys who treat you like a little girl.

Once you heal, you will be able to empathize with others without sacrificing yourself for them.

Do your inner work!

Number Twenty-Four...

You're not learning from your mistakes.

First you must pull up your grown woman panties and admit that this relationship was a mistake in the first place.

Then know that just because you made a mistake, doesn't mean you have to see it through.

Stop thinking the stars will magically align and the outcome will be different this time.

It won't be.

Clearly identify the role you are playing in perpetuating these relationships by trying to stick it out.

It is okay to admit defeat for your own self-preservation.

Seek outside perspective if you need to because sometimes, we are too close to a problem to see it.

Do something. Make a move. Stop acting like you don't have choices.

Because you do.

Sometimes the learning hurts.

Number Twenty-Five...

You don't trust that you can choose someone good for you.

Most of us have been shell-shocked by atrocious relationships, especially if you were used or abused.

And I get it…you're scared to repeat the same mistakes and end up with someone who doesn't treat you right.

The good thing about learning from mistakes is we become more cautious with who we date and how we date.

But it's still scary to step into the dating ring to test out how ready we are, right?

This is how you learn to trust yourself:

Know your triggers – red flags, hurtful comments and anything that sets you off.

Trust your gut – don't obsess about "maybe he didn't mean it."

Don't feel guilty – don't waste your time on forgiveness.

Do not give an inch on your standards – do NOT fight with him about treating you better.

144

If he sets your radar off, cut him down like a tree and don't look back while he's falling.

PRACTICE. ZERO. TOLERANCE.

See, women are made to feel guilty about not sticking around to help a male work through his shit.

I believe that forgiveness is a gaslighting tactic to let someone shit on you again.

He is NOT 'a great guy.' If he was, he wouldn't be triggering you.

Let him fight his own demons…on his own.

Number Twenty-Six…

You are stuck in a cycle of emotional abuse.

From personal experience, I know that it's very hard to get out of an emotionally abusive relationship.

Emotional abuse is insidious; it's gradual and subtle but with very harmful effects.

Sometimes the abuser is so manipulative that you don't even realize you're being abused.

And many women don't recognize abuse when there are no physical scars.

With emotional abuse the cycle of ups and downs unfortunately becomes confusing and addictive.

Your confusion is what he's counting on because he can more easily convince you that you deserve his abusive behavior.

He will also try to convince you that you are imagining things or taking him the wrong way.

Clean breaks and lots of space will help you detach from this merry-go-round of despair.

A clean break, or going no contact, is hard to do because he's so charming when he's making things up to you.

This is done to keep you off balance too.

It's called love bombing and it won't last.

He's manipulating you by giving you the attention and affection you crave 99% of the time, but that he rarely gives.

As soon as he retrains you to accept his bare minimum efforts, the cycle will start again.

Get off the ride!

Number Twenty-Seven…

You think he has potential.

So, he has potential, huh?

According to whom might I ask?

Because the fact is he's had that same level of potential since he was born.

Just like you and I have.

Lack of potential means lack of funds.

Why should you settle for the "potential of potential," when he gets to benefit from the crème de la crème right now?

It's okay to know that he is not good enough for you.

And it's okay to admit that he is way out of his league.

Instead of birthing his dreams (and potential), choose someone who is on your level, or higher.

Women don't get to use the excuse of having potential.

We are called gold diggers if we date at levels above where we are.

If it's broke, don't feed it.

Number Twenty-Eight…

You're attracted to emotionally unavailable males.

Ever met someone, hit it off at record speed, then spent the rest of the "relationship" pissed off because he was now acting indifferent and cold.

You feel off balance because things were going so well at first.

Therefore, you start to think "maybe it's me… what did I do wrong?"

So, you start trying to get that initial newness and magic back. You start trying to be what he wants again.

But the more you try, the more you get shut down, rebuffed, or rejected.

These males are aware of the mind games that they play. You will do well to remember this.

But also…let him play with his mama.

Number Twenty-Nine…

You're emotionally unavailable yourself.

The more we settle for deprived males, the more detrimental we become to ourselves.

You cannot be in an emotionally unavailable relationship and not become emotionally unavailable yourself because your instincts to protect yourself will kick in.

Shut yourself off to being bothered by his lack of emotional support and overall shenanigans.

It is also possible that you are choosing males who emotionally reject or abandon you because you had an unstable male figure in your life.

These are attractions of deprivation, none of which you deserve.

Number Thirty…

You want the breakup misery to stop.

You go back, not because you are seeing any positive changes in him, but because you want the misery of the breakup withdrawals to stop.

Your misery with him has become the norm. The pain and hurt of being apart forces you to go back to the norm.

Studies show that we crave a lost partner like a drug addict craves drugs.

In other words, it's a chemical reaction.

It's a chemical fix like that of a drug addict craving drugs.

So, you rationalize your choice to stay by convincing yourself that he's worth the misery.

He's not.

Detox.

These thirty reasons are the symptoms of patriarchy, misogyny, and sexism.

They are what women have been conditioned to accept for centuries.

While you can't change the world's view, you can change YOUR WORLDVIEW.

Let's get off the "struggle love" bus.

Love is NOT pain.

Love is love.

And pain is pain.

Made in the USA
Columbia, SC
06 July 2022

62941591R00087